Contents

Composer's note

Creation Song was written as a response to a request from Ashley Grote, the Master of Music at Norwich Cathedral, along with Canon Aidan Platten from the Dean and Chapter. Norwich Cathedral was due to be the final stop on a nationwide British tour, which began in February 2018, of the replica skeleton of 'Dippy' the dinosaur from the Natural History Museum in London. The idea was to celebrate this visit to Norwich with a piece that could be sung by the Cathedral Choir along with a large choir of schoolchildren. The resulting work, *Creation Song*, is scored for upper voices, SATB, and organ. It is written in sections with a recurring refrain but is designed to be sung as a continuous piece. The opening tempo marking suggests a speed that remains constant throughout, but please feel free to allow for some flexibility of tempo in certain sections if that feels right to you. The refrain, written for upper voices, can equally be sung by the mixed choir in any voice combination that you may choose should an upper-voice choir not be available. I am grateful to both Ashley Grote and Canon Aidan Platten, as well as the Norfolk Music Hub, for the commitment, energy, and enthusiasm that they have shown towards this lovely project.

Duration: *c*.12 minutes

A lyric sheet and separate part for the upper voices is available for free download from the catalogue page of the OUP website.

Creation Song

Bob Chilcott

for upper voices, SATB, and organ

vocal score

MUSIC DEPARTMENT

OXFORD
UNIVERSITY PRESS

OXFORD
UNIVERSITY PRESS

Great Clarendon Street, Oxford OX2 6DP,
United Kingdom

Oxford University Press is a department of the University of Oxford.
It furthers the University's objective of excellence in research, scholarship,
and education by publishing worldwide. Oxford is a registered trade mark of
Oxford University Press in the UK and in certain other countries

First published 2021

Impression: 1

ISBN 978-0-19-354586-1

Music and text origination by Katie Johnston
Printed in Great Britain on acid-free paper by
Halstan & Co. Ltd, Amersham, Bucks.

Commissioned by the Dean and Chapter of Norwich Cathedral with generous support from the Norfolk Music Hub,
for the Natural History Museum's 'Dippy on Tour' exhibition in Norwich,
and in celebration of the beauty of creation as the world seeks a sustainable future.

Creation Song

BOB CHILCOTT

Movement 1

Genesis 1: 1–5 (adap.)

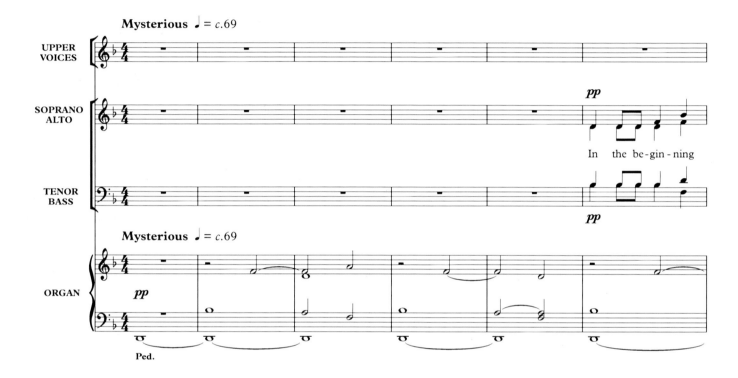

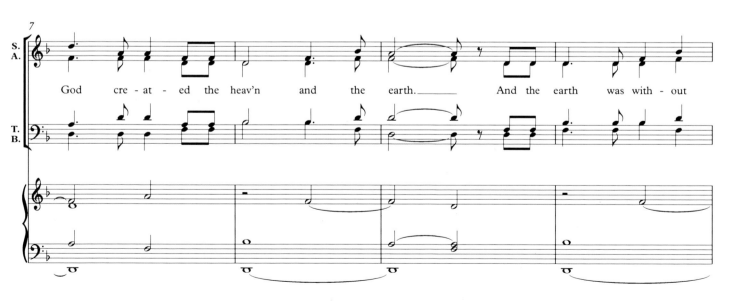

form,_____ and void,_____ void;_____ and dark-ness was up-on the

face of the deep,_____ deep._____ And God

said, Let there be light: and there was light.

attacca

Refrain 1

Thomas Traherne (*c.*1637–1674)

attacca

Movement 2

Joseph Addison (1672–1719)

attacca

Refrain 2

Thomas Traherne (*c.*1637–1674)

attacca

Movement 3

Isaac Watts (1674–1748)

sing the good-ness of the Lord, who filled the earth with

I sing the good-ness of the Lord, who filled the earth with

food, who formed the crea-tures through the Word, and

food, who formed the crea-tures through the Word,

then pro-nounced them good, good, good.

and then pro-nounced them good, good, good.

attacca

Refrain 3

Thomas Traherne (*c.*1637–1674)

attacca

Movement 4

Gerard Manley Hopkins (1844–89)

Look,___ look at the stars!___ The bright bo - roughs, the cir - cle -

-ci - ta - dels___ there, cir - cle - ci - ta - dels___ there!___ Look at the

stars,___ look at the stars,_____ the___ stars!_____

attacca

Refrain 4

Thomas Traherne (*c*.1637–1674)

attacca

Movement 5

Emily Dickinson (1830–86)

Refrain 5

Thomas Traherne (*c.*1637–1674)

The earth, the seas,_ the light, the day, the skies,___ the earth, the seas,_ the light, the day, the skies,___ the_ skies, The_ sun and stars_ are mine, the_ sun and stars_ are mine, if those I prize.

attacca

Movement 6

Thomas Traherne (*c.*1637–1674)

attacca

Refrain 6

Thomas Traherne (*c.*1637–1674)